MW00772173

Dwelling in the Presence
OF THE DIVINE

Dwelling in the Presence of the Divine, A Commonplace Book of the Hebrew Living™ Letters by Robin Main ©2023
All rights reserved.

First Edition.

Sapphire Throne Ministries
Loveland, Colorado
SapphireThroneMinistries.com

 | Managing Editor: Robin Shukle
Design: Liz Mrofka,
whatifpublishing.com

Printed by: Kindle Direct Publishing

ISBN: 978-0-9985982-7-7

Dwelling in the Presence
OF THE DIVINE

A COMMONPLACE BOOK
OF THE
HEBREW LIVING™ LETTERS

ROBIN MAIN

AN INVITATION

The mysterious Hebrew phrase on the back cover (אֶת־פָּנֶיךָ שֹׂבַע שְׂמָחוֹת) is a divine invitation into the fullness of joy in ALEF-TAV (את)'s Presence. Its voice comes from Psalms 16:11. One glorious facet of the Almighty's Dwelling Presence is His delightful living letters from ALEF (א) to TAV (ת).

Just as a home is a common place for a family to gather, so may this commonplace book be for ALEF-TAV (את)'s letters. Just as we scrapbook our valued memories, so may this Commonplace Book of Hebrew Living™ Letters be. Historically, commonplace books have provided an effective way to collect various thoughts, experiences, quotes, Bible verses, or anything that you would like to retain and remember about a topic—in one place. The book becomes a "commonplace" for you to collect your nuggets of wisdom, information you may want to experience or access again.

There are four components for each of the 22 sections— one section for each Hebrew letter, which are meant to assist you in *Dwelling in the Presence of the Divine.* Each section creates a space to interact with the unique energy and extraordinary character of each Hebrew letter as well as forming within you a flexible, ever-expanding container for ALEF-TAV (את)'s immense limitless riches.

≈ Notice how the four heavenly components take you on an exploratory journey where you will first encounter the basics of a Hebrew letter.

≈ Then, you are shown a pillar of truth about that living letter in which you are encouraged to meditate upon under a canopy of love, kindness, and joy before walking it out.

≈ After that are several blank pages provided so you can collect your treasures about a Hebrew letter. Perhaps, a thought strikes you. Or you get a light bulb moment revelation. Or a quote or Bible verse is highlighted to you. Take note and write it down in this commonplace book to lock it in your memory, which will also help keep track of the things that are important to you.

≈ Finally, there is one last uplifting letter whisper from ALEF-TAV (את) to promote His splendid revelation-light within you.

May your sublime soul delight in ALEF-TAV (את) and His Creation's joy and glory from ALEF(א) to TAV (ת).

TABLE OF CONTENTS

ALEF

(ah - lef)

Ox. Bull.

Strength. Leader. First.

Sound — Silent

is the letter of fire—
AYSH/ESH (אֵשׁ)
—which is the substance
that consumes the sacrifice.
Fundamentally, fire
represents the Presence of
God, as revealed to Moses
in the burning bush and in
the Pillar of Fire protecting
His people in the wilderness.
Behold, אֵשׁ is the light,
heat, energy, and power of
transformation of a burning
heart who loves the LORD
God with all their heart,
soul, and strength.

*B*lessed is the one
whose burning heart
embraces the fiery presence
of YHVH's **ALEF** (א).

BET

(bet)

Tent. House.

Household. Family. "In."

Sound — b as in boy.

---

is a house firmly set on earth.
The dot in the middle of בּ
is called a dagesh, which
represents one who lives within.
Jacob was the man whose head
rested upon the Rock where he
had a vivid dream of a ladder
reaching up from earth to
heaven with angels ascending
and descending on it. God
proclaimed to Jacob, *"Behold,
I am with you and will keep you
wherever you go" (Gen. 28:15).*
The ladder to the gate of heaven
was Jacob's own DNA, having
been made in God's own image.
Behold, God is with you, and you
are the House of God.

בּ

ב

ב

*B*lessed is the one who makes room within to fully become the Almighty's beloved **BET (ב)** home.

GIMEL

(geeh-mel)

Camel.

To lift up. Pride. Provision.

Sound — g as in God.

ג

is the letter of bestowing
lovingkindness—GIMILUT
HASIDIM. (גְּמִילוּת חֲסָדִים)
Lovingkindness leaves an
eternal mark upon the place
that it's performed as well as
elevating people to
heavenly levels.

ג

ג

ג

ג

*B*lessed is the one
whose **GIMEL (ג)'s**
portion is lovingkindness.

DALET

(dah-let)

Door.

Poor Man. Elevation.

Sound — d as in Day.

ד

is the door for His sheep. On the
night when God brought out His
people from Egypt (the world)
with a mighty hand and
outstretched arm, they were
instructed to put the blood
DAHM (דָּם) of the Passover Lamb
on their door DELET (דֶּלֶת),
which represented entrance to
the home of their heart.

ד

ד

*B*lessed is the one who opens the DALET (ד) door to the four chambers of their heart to His delightful and glorious Kingdom within.

HEI

(hay)

Behold.

To reveal. To show. "The."

Sound — h as in hay.

ה

is the letter of the most
effortless sound a soul can
make . . . taking a breath. That is
why there is some of ה in every
word and why it seems so
unfathomable for it is the sound
of being present—HAYAH (הָיָה).
Hey! God says to each of us:
EHYEH ASHER EHYEH
(אֶהְיֶה אֲשֶׁר אֶהְיֶה)
"I will be what I will be" (Exo. 3:14).
Not who you want me to be.
To be is to exist, to abide,
to remain, to continue,
to accompany, and to occur.

ה

ה

ה

ה

*B*lessed is the one
who is present with
every **HEI** (ה) breath.

VAV

(vahv)

Nail. Peg.

To add. To secure. "and."

Sound — v as in vase.

ו

is the sound of being joined;
because it is the sound of the
word "and." Behold, God created
the heavens ו the earth. One can
only join another if they are
both distinct; otherwise, one
would absorb the other. This is
not the way of unity. The work
of VAV is to join us all into a
myriad of constellations where
we each remain unique, yet we
are bound to each other being
one in Christ.

ו

*B*lessed is the one who is **VAV (ו)**—joined to the Father of lights and receives every good and perfect gift that comes from above.

ZAYIN

(ZAH-yeen)

Weapon. Sword. To cut. To pierce.

Sound — z as in Zion.

ז

is the letter of a sword and a
seed ZERA (זֶרַע). The sword of the
Spirit, which is the Word of God,
has seven flaming flows . . . the
Spirit of the Lord, the Spirit of
Wisdom, the Spirit of
Understanding, the Spirit of
Counsel, the Spirit of Might, the
Spirit of Knowledge, and the
Spirit of the Fear of the Lord.
These Seven Spirits of God
contain the incorruptible seed
of the Word of God.

ז

*B*lessed is the one who receives the fullness of **ZAYIN (ז)**'s incorruptible seed.

CHET

(Rhymes with "met")

To protect. To separate.

Sound — ch as in Bach.

is an acronym for "life"—CHAIM
(חַיִּים). The human body is
brought to life when the
Seven Spirits of God infused soul
(נְשָׁמָה) enters a person's body.
Throughout our lives,
we physically exist mostly as water.
Behold, in the midst of
the Kingdom of God within you
is the pure river of the water
of life that comes from
His Throne with the Tree of Life
on either side.

*B*lessed is the one
who flows in
CHET (ח)'s water of life.

TET

(Rhymes with "mate")

To surround. To twist.

Sound — t as in tall.

ט

is good—TOV (טוב). Not only does טוב mean to be good, but it also signifies to be pleasing, to be beneficial, to be delightful, and to be favorable. The sweet psalmist of Israel—King David—tells us that we can taste and see that the Lord is good. The earth is full of His goodness. The goodness of God endures forever. The LORD delights in the steps of every good person, and we are satisfied with the goodness of His house, which the LORD surrounds and makes secure.

ט

ত

ט

*B*lessed is the one who tastes and sees all the goodness of **TET** (ט).

י

YUD

(yood)

To make. To work. Deed done.

Sound — y as in yes.

ר

is like a dove—YONA (יוֹנָה)—which
descends from heaven to gently
alight and remain on His pleasing ones,
just like the Pattern Son who is the
Son of God. Those who adore Him have
the singleness of vision of dove eyes
with an olive branch in their mouth,
proclaiming the good tidings of peace
that surpasses all understanding.

ר

ר

*B*lessed is the one who receives the sparks of **YUD** (י), which brings singleness of vision and the peace that surpasses all understanding.

KAF

(kaf)

To open. To cover. To allow.

Sound — k as in kite.

is the palm of the hand filled with
sincerity—KAVANAH (כַּוָּנָה)—which
reveals a prayer life of depth and
meaning. To kavanah is to pray with
purpose and sincerity where your
heart and mind are engaged in the
act of coming before the King of
Kings and the Lord of all Creation.
Mindful, sincere prayers happen
through ones who focus on what
is the good, the pleasing,
and the perfect will of the Father.
Always remember that prayer is
a conversation, so the power of
prayer includes listening
as well as speaking.

כ

*B*lessed is the one whose palm is filled with **KAF (כ)** sincerity, which contains glorious depth and profound meaning.

LAMED

(lah-med)

To prod. To go forward. To control.

Sound — l as in lion.

ל

is tall and beautiful. It represents
the heart—LEV (לֵב)—of the
Good Shepherd who offers a
resting place in His luxurious love
and who guides His flock to a
wonderful oasis of peace.

ל

ל

ל

ל

ל

*B*lessed is the one
who surrenders
wholeheartedly to the
LAMED (ל) guidance
of the Good Shepherd.

MEM

(mem)

Liquid. Mighty & Massive. Chaos.

Sound — m as in mother.

מ

is the physical substance that
Earth has been founded. This is
the water—MAYIM (מַיִם)—and
this is the wilderness—MIDBAR
(מִדְבָּר)—that we wander and are
made ready to enter the
Promise Land.

מ

מ

מ

מ

*B*lessed is the one who receives the refreshing living waters of **MEM** (מ) in every area of their life.

NUN

(noon)

Action. Activity. Life.

Sound — n as in now.

נ

is the living soul—N'SHAMAH
(נְשָׁמָה)—that God created in His
own image through the breath
of the Almighty. Each soul—
NEFESH (נֶפֶשׁ)—closes one's eyes
to see the cascading wonders
NIFL'LAOT (נפלאות) of נ. NUN (נ) is
the holy spark—NITZOTZ
(ניצוץ)—in each one of us, which
burns brighter as we are
faithful—NE'EMAN (נֶאֱמָן).

נ

*B*lessed is the one
who gathers the
cascading wonders
of **NUN (נ)**.

SAMECH

(sah-mekh)

Support. Shield.

Sound — s as in sin.

is dwelling in the harvest hut
of the SUKKAH (סֻכָּה), which
reminds us of God's supreme
and supernatural shelter in
the Wilderness of Sinai (סיני).
Only the One who
gave you life can keep it.
Lean into the peace that the
shelter of SAMECH (ס) brings.

ס

*B*lessed is the one
who has the full
support and peaceful shelter
of the Almighty's **SAMECH** (ס).

AYIN

(ah-yeen)

To see. To turn aside. Twist slowly.

Sound — silent.

is an eye—AYIN (עַיִן)—that sees
but doesn't speak. עַ reveals the
wondrous and silent humility—
ANAVAH (עֲנָוָה)—of serving the
Creator. To AVODAH (עֲבוֹדָה) is to
work, to worship, and to serve.
God's original design in
Genesis 2:15 illustrates that
our work and our worship
are a seamless way of living.

עַ

ע

ע

ע

ע

ע

*B*lessed is the one who who sees with piercing **AYIN** (ע) sight.

PEY

(pay)

To speak. To understand. To know.

Sound — p as in pastor.

פ

is the mouth that first speaks
the simple, plain sense truth—
P'SHAT (פשט). However,
everything conceals a myriad
of layers, for everything is
a miracle—PELE (פֶּלֶא).
There is an orchard—PAR'DES
(פַּרְדֵּס)—that belongs to the
righteous whose fruit—P'RIY
(פְּרִי)—is the wisdom of all
which is hidden.

*B*lessed is the one whose mouth pours forth **PEY (פ)**'s praises.

TZADIK

(tsah-dee)

To pull toward. Desire. Harvest.

Sound — ts as in boots.

צ

is righteousness—TZEDEK (צֶדֶק).
The righteous and the humble
shall inherit the Earth. The
righteous deeds of the saints
clothes the Bride of the Messiah
(Rev. 19:7-8) whose faith is set
like flint upon the Rock—TZUR
(צוּר)—that is higher than
themselves. Their goal is the joy
of the whole earth, which is the
True North of the holy hill of
TZIYON (צִיּוֹן).

צ

צ

צ

*B*lessed is the one
whose heart points
to Zion where the righteousness
of **TSADIK (צ)** dwells.

KOOF

(kof)

Surround. Great strength. Holy.

Sound — q as in queen.

ק

is the call of holy—KADOSH
(שׁוֹדק). KOOF (ק) is the voice—
KOL (לוֹק)—of a person
proclaiming the oneness and
the glory of God. ק is the
infinite worship before the
Throne: *"Holy, holy, holy,
Lord God Almighty" (Rev. 4:8).*

ק

*B*lessed is the one
who hears the
KOOF (ק)'s call of holy and
joins its infinite worship of the
Most High God.

RESH

(raysh)

A person.   What is highest.

Sound — r as in run.

ר

is ultimately about being closer
to the Head—ROSH (רֹאשׁ)—of
the Body of the Messiah than to
anyone else. We speak the truth
in love, so all things may grow
up and attach correctly to the
Head; thus, we hold fast to the
Head that nourishes and
sustains the Body of Christ.

ר

*B*lessed is the one who speaks the

RESH (ר) truth in love.

SHIN

(sheen)

To devour. To destroy. To consume.

Sound — s as in sin.

שׁ

is the sound of the SHOFAR (שׁוֹפָר) that gathers all the broken pieces. It is the SHALOM (שָׁלוֹם) peace that breaks the authority of chaos and brings wholeness; and thus, ushers in the rest of the seventh day SHABBAT (שַׁבָּת) where the divine presence dwells— SHEKINAH (שְׁכִינָה).

ש

ש

ש

*B*lessed is the one who enters the shalom, shabbat, and shekinah of **SHIN** (ש).

TAV

(tav)

Ownership. To seal. To make a sign.

Sound — t as in toy.

is the name for a prayerful call
to God—TEFILA (תפילה). TAV (ת)
is the name for singing God's
praises through psalm—TEHILIM
(תְּהִלִּים). TAV (ת) is the sound of
returning to God through
repentance—TESHUVAH
(תְּשׁוּבָה), which leads to the
repairing of the Universe—
TIKKUN (תִּקּוּן).

ת

ת

ת

ת

ת

ת

*B*lessed is the one
whose heart bows
with the teshuvah of **TAV (ת)**,
which leads to the repairing
of their universe.

ABOUT THE AUTHOR

Robin Main is a prophetic artist, author, speaker, teacher and mentor who equips people to be the unique and beautiful creation that they have been created to be. She flows in love, revelation and wisdom with her SPECIALTY being kingdom enlightenment.

Her MISSION is to enlighten the nations by venturing to educate and restore the sons of the Living God.

Her CALL is a clarion one to mature sons, and the pure and spotless Bride of Christ who will indeed be without spot or wrinkle.

Her ULTIMATE DESIRE is that everyone be rooted and grounded in love, so they can truly know the height, width, breadth and depth of the Heavenly Father's love.

OTHER BOOKS BY ROBIN MAIN

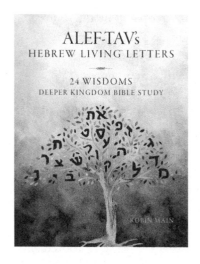 

This Dwelling in the Presence of the Divine:
A Commonplace Book of the Hebrew Living™ Letters is
designed to be a companion to *ALEF-TAV's Hebrew*
Living™ Letters Bible Study and *Quantum 22™*.
However, these presence-filled pages
can be enjoyed all by themselves.
Please feel free to flow by the Spirit of the Living God.

Additional books by Robin Main can be found at
sapphirethroneministries.com

*B*lessed
is the one
who knows
ALEF-TAV (תא).

Made in the USA
Las Vegas, NV
11 November 2024

11628112R00105